COLETTE *Barbara Diestzsch* WALT WHITMAN *Hokusai* FRANCES EL

XON *Vincent van Gogh* THE ODES OF SOL GERTR

t ALFRED, LORD TENNYSON *Walter Crane* *Thor*

y *Victor Higgins* ROBERT FRANCIS *Geor* ADDIS

atisse ROBERT FROST *Henri Fantin-Latour* ELEANOUR SINCLAIR RO

Ehret HELÉNE CIXOUS *Barbara Diestzsch* HENRY DAVID THOREAU *He*

Jean François Millet WALT WHITMAN *Hokusai* FRANCES ELIZA HODGS

ent *van Gogh* THE ODES OF SOLOMON *Girolamo Pini* GERTRUDE JEK

ED, LORD TENNYSON *Walter Crane* VIRGINIA WOOLF *R. J. Thorton* WU-N

iggins ROBERT FRANCIS *Georgia O'Keeffe* JOSEPH ADDISON *W. Thort*

t FROST *Henri Fantin-Latour* ELEANOUR SINCLAIR ROHDE *Gusta*

LÉNE CIXOUS *Barbara Diestzsch* HENRY DAVID THOREAU *Hokusai* FRAN

ALAN DIXON *Vincent van Gogh* THE ODES OF SOLOMON *Girolamo P*

ouard *Manet* ALFRED, LORD TENNYSON *Walter Crane* VIRGINIA WOO

et EDWARD ABBEY *Victor Higgins* ROBERT FRANCIS *Georgia O'Keef*

ck *Henri Matisse* ROBERT FROST *Henri Fantin-Latour* ELEANO

stave Caillebotte RUBÉN DARÍO Sandro Botticelli PABLO NER

D. Ehret COLETTE Barbara Diestzsch WALT WHITMAN Hokusai FRAN

ZA HODGSON BURNETT J. Stella EDNA ST. VINCENT MILLAY Jacopo Ligo

N DIXON Vincent van Gogh THE ODES OF SOLOMON Girolamo P

TRUDE JEKYLL Osias Beert IZUMI SHIKIBU Hokusai EDITH WHAR

ouard Manet ALFRED, LORD TENNYSON Walter Crane VIRGINIA WO

J. Thorton WU-MEN William Sharp ANNE SEXTON Jean-Franc

billet EDWARD ABBEY Victor Higgins ROBERT FRANCIS Georgia O'Kee

EPH ADDISON W. Thorton KOKUZO OKAKURA Henri Matisse ROBERT FR

enri Fantin-Latour ELEANOUR SINCLAIR ROHDE Gustave Caillebo

ANE ACKERMAN Sandro Botticelli LEWIS CARROLL G. D. Ehret HEI

KOUS Barbara Diestzsch HENRY DAVID THOREAU Henri Matisse RU

RÍO Sandro Botticelli PABLO NERUDA Edouard Manet COL

ictor Higgins WALT WHITMAN Hokusai FRANCES ELIZA HODGSON BURN

Stella EDNA ST. VINCENT MILLAY Jacopo Ligozzi ALAN DIXON Vinc

n Gogh THE ODES OF SOLOMON Girolamo Pini GERTRUDE JEKYLL Os

THE CULTIVATED

GARDENER

Flowers

Edited by Kristin Joyce

A SWANS ISLAND BOOK

CollinsPublishersSanFrancisco
A Division of HarperCollinsPublishers

Published in 1996 by
Collins Publishers San Francisco
1160 Battery Street
San Francisco, California 94111

Produced by Swans Island Books, Inc.
Belvedere, California 94920

Book design by Madeleine Corson Design
with special gratitude to Madeleine and Ann.

Additional thanks to:
Laurie Platt Winfrey and Robin Sand of Carousel Research, Inc.
Shellei Addison of Flying Fish Books
Julie Nathan of Swans Island Books

Library of Congress Cataloging-in-Publication Data
Flowers/ edited by Kristin Joyce
p. cm. – (The Cultivated gardener)
"A Swans Island book,"
Includes index.
ISBN 0-00-225050-0
I. Flowers – Quotations, maxims, etc.
I. Joyce, Kristin. II. Series
PN6084. F5F465 1996
582. 13' O4166 – dc20   95-11930
Printed in Italy
1 3 5 7 9 10 8 6 4 2

"An almanac religion connects us to a flower." As Colette's observation suggests, we might better understand and appreciate the sacred cycles of living as we do the ephemeral bloom. What exists before us is so fleeting, yet eternal. Petals of light, pure color, and exotic scent, are all deeply etched upon the human memory for decades. Seasons, even years, compress within days as the effulgent bud awakens with morning dew, blossoms in noonday sun, withers by twilight. Thus, the many *flowers* of this anthology, by their fragile yet powerful nature, enlighten and connect us to the moment and all time. ❧ These many talented writers and artists construct vivid portrayals of love linked to floral fragrance or sensual color. Diane Ackerman recounts Napoleon's fetish for Josephine's "natural aromas" infused with the scent of violets; Louise Glück describes an erotic "churning sea of poppies" surrounding her lovers "who make a garden between them like a bed of stars," and Colette — whose writings on flowers alone comprise entire tomes — offers the fragrant peony "which has the privilege of putting us in touch with the true spring, bearer of many suspect odors, the sum of which is likely to leave us enchanted." ❧ While flowers recollect these erotic or bittersweet images, they also impart tremendous peace and universal joy. "A morning glory at my window satisfies me more than the metaphysics of books," states Walt Whitman. Kokuzo Okakura tells us, "In joy or sadness, flowers are our constant friends. We eat, drink, sing, dance and flirt with them." Surely there is great flirtation, dancing and singing as expressed in the fine art of Thorton's "Temple of Flora" tulips, the grand hues of van Gogh's irises and sunflowers, the botanical detail of Redouté's roses, or Botticelli's supremely beautiful "The Spring," which still represents one of the most elaborate works on flowers. ⤢ *The Cultivated Gardener: Flowers,* is one in a series of four books which includes single subject anthologies on *Fruits, Vegetables* and *Trees.* Each volume celebrates the gardens, both wild and tame, which cross every field of human endeavor and unite us with the world of nature. It is almost unfathomable, however, to imagine editing the breadth of beautiful and intelligent work which exists to date. Skimming this immense sea of flowers to fill ninety-six pages was my one true sadness. And then I came across the wisdom of Wu-men: "Ten thousand flowers in spring, the moon in autumn, a cool breeze in summer, snow in winter, If your mind isn't clouded by unnecessary things, this is the best season of your life." ⤢ As you turn these pages, may you experience ten thousand flowers in spring.

⤢ *K.J.*

An almanac religion connects us to a flower,...

And the flowers
were fresh and lovely,
        drenched with fragrance: the virgin rose,
        the white daisy,
                the gracious lily and the morning-glories
                that hang from the shaken branch.
                        And I said, "M o r e..."

RUBÉN DARÍO

I do not love you as if you were salt-rose, or topaz,
or the arrow of carnations the fire shoots off.

I love you as certain dark things are to be loved,
in secret, between the shadow and the soul.

I love you as the plant that never blooms
but carries in itself the light of hidden flowers;

thanks to your love a certain solid fragrance,
risen from the earth, lives darkly in my body.

PABLO NERUDA

An almanac religion connects us to a flower,
even a puny one,
when it symbolizes a season,
to its color
when it commemorates a saint,
to its scent
if it painfully takes us back
to a lost bliss.

COLETTE

A morning-glory
at my window
satisfies me more than
the metaphysics of books.

WALT WHITMAN

I accidentally praised a tulip as one of the finest I ever saw;
upon which they told me it was a common Fool's Coat.

Upon that I praised a second, which it seems was but another
kind of Fool's Coat.... *The gentleman smiled at my ignorance.*

He seemed a very plain honest man, and a person of good
sense, had not his head been touched with that distemper
which Hippocrates calls the Tulippomania; insomuch that

he would talk very rationally on any subject
in the world but a tulip.

JOSEPH ADDISON

16/17

All my heart became a tear,
All my soul became a tower,
Never loved I anything
As I loved that tall blue flower!

It was all the little boats
That had ever sailed the sea,
It was all the little books
That had gone to school with me;

On its roots like iron claws
Rearing up so blue and tall —
It was all the gallant Earth
With its back against the wall!

EDNA ST. VINCENT MILLAY

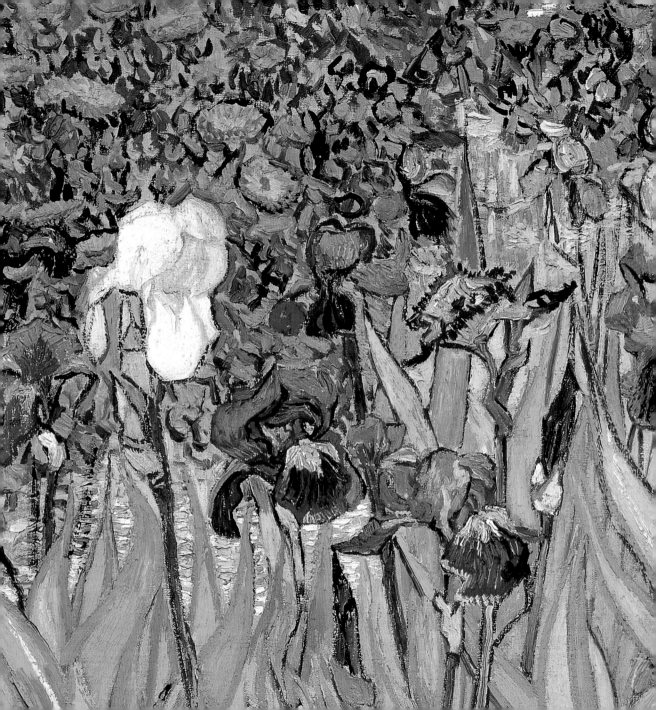

I can hear the iris blossom. Its last protective silken layer
rasps and splits down the length of an azure finger which *u n c o i l s*
at the proper time and, sitting by oneself in a small quiet room,
one may start suddenly if one has forgotten that, on a nearby table,
an iris has suddenly decided to *b l o s s o m.*

Consider how there are, at the Cours-la-Reine, thousands of irises,
renewed by continued flowering. The early morning sun delivers those
whose time is come and I am seized with desire for that morning when,

        in the dawn that filters through the curtains,
        I may be able to cock an ear for the perceptible
        sighing of so many irises *d e l i v e r e d* simultaneously....

                   COLETTE

Blessed
are the men and women who are
planted on your earth, in your garden,
who grow as your trees and flowers grow,
who transform their darkness to light.
Their roots plunge into darkness;
their faces turn toward the light.

THE ODES OF SOLOMON

Nothing can be more absolutely unscientific than
my ways, according to the usual sense of the word....
In gardening I try to paint living pictures with
living flowers, paying attention to throwing them into
groups both for form and colour, and so on.
I am perpetually at amicable war with the
gardener for over-trimness. His grand idea is that
edges must be trimmed, and all walks brushed every Saturday,
while I hold the heresy of not minding a
little moss on a path, and of rather preferring
a few scattered cluster rose-petals lying on its
brown-green velvet.

GERTRUDE JEKYLL

As I dig
for wild orchids
in the autumn fields,
it is the deeply-bedded
root that I desire,
not the flower.

IZUMI SHIKIBU

28/29

Though it is an exaggeration to say that there are no
flowers in Italian gardens, yet to enjoy and appreciate the Italian garden-craft
one must always bear in mind that it is independent of floriculture.

The Italian garden does not exist for flowers; its flowers exist for it
They are a late and infrequent adjunct to its beauties,
a parenthetical grace counting only as one more touch
in the general effect of enchantment.

This is no doubt partly explained by the difficulty of
cultivating any but spring flowers in so hot and dry a climate,
and the result has been a wonderful development of the more
permanent effects to be obtained from the three other factors in
garden-composition – marble, water and perennial verdure –
and the achievement, by their skillful blending,
of a charm independent of the seasons.

EDITH WHARTON

...the most beautiful individual flower, most people would agree,
is that of the cacti: the prickly pear, the hedgehog, the fishhook.

Merely opinion, of course. But the various cactus flowers have earned
the distinction claimed for them on the basis of their large size,
their delicacy, their brilliance, and their transience —

they bloom, many of them, for one day only in each year.
Is that a fair criterion of beauty? I don't know.
For myself I hold no preference among flowers,
so long as they are w i l d,   f r e e,   s p o n t a n e o u s.

EDWARD ABBEY

The Peony
has the privilege of putting us in touch
with the true spring, bearer of many suspect odors,
the sum of which is likely to leave us
e n c h a n t e d.

COLETTE

The rose is a rose.

And was always a rose.

But the theory now goes

That the apple's a rose,

And the pear is, and so's

The plum, I suppose.

The dear only knows

What will next prove a rose.

You, of course, are a rose —

But were always a rose.

ROBERT FROST

…all is permitted
t h e   r o s e —
splendor, a conspiracy of
perfumes, petalous flesh
that tempts the nose,
the lips, the teeth.

COLETTE

The rose sleeps in her beauty, but the lily
seems unaware of her own exceeding loveliness.
The rose is never so glorious as in cultivation
and fares sumptuously, with every care lavished on her
        but, given rich food instead of the sharp drainage
        and leaf mould to which she is accustomed,
        the lily withdraws her gracious presence.
                The purity of the lily is not only in her outward form,
                but it is characteristic of the food she requires.
                No members of the lily family tolerate manure,
                artificial or otherwise.
                        The lily is at her fairest
                        in the waste places of the earth,
                        where human eyes rarely see her in her beauty.

ELEANOUR SINCLAIR ROHDE

And then, opening her eyes, how *f r e s h* like frilled linen
clean from a laundry laid in wicker trays the roses looked;
and dark and prim the red carnations, holding their heads up; and
all the sweet peas spreading in their bowls, tinged violet, snow whit
pale – as if it were the evening and girls in muslin frocks came out
to pick the sweet peas and roses after the superb summer's day,

with its almost blue-black sky, its delphiniums,

its carnations, its arum lilies was over; and it was the moment

between six and seven when every flower — roses, carnations, irises, lilac — glows;

white, violet, red, deep orange;

every flower seems to burn by itself, softly, purely

in the misty beds;...

VIRGINIA WOOLF

In a famous letter, Napoleon told Josephine
"not to bathe" during the two weeks that would pass
before they met, so that he could enjoy all her natural aromas.
            But Napoleon and Josephine also adored violets.
            She often wore a violet-scented perfume, which was her trademark.
            When she died in 1814, Napoleon planted violets at her grave.
                        Just before his exile on St. Helena, he made a pilgrimage to it,
                        picked some of the violets, and entombed them in a locket,
                        which he wore around his neck;
                                    they stayed there until the end of his life.

DIANE ACKERMAN

Ten thousand flowers in spring,
the moon in autumn, a cool breeze in summer, snow in winter.
If your mind isn't clouded by unnecessary things,
this is the best season of your life.

WU-MEN

This time she came upon a large flower-bed, with a
border of daisies, and a willow-tree growing in the middle.

'O Tiger-lily,' said Alice, addressing herself to one that
was waving gracefully about in the wind, 'I wish you could talk!'

'We can talk,' said the Tiger-lily: 'when there's anybody worth talking to.'

Alice was so astonished that she couldn't speak for a minute:
it quite seemed to take her breath away. At length, as the Tiger-lily
only went on waving about, she spoke again, in a timid voice –
almost in a whisper.

'And can all the flowers talk?'

'As well as you can,' said the Tiger-lily.

'And a great deal louder.'

LEWIS CARROLL

In the garden,
I found out the secret:
There are flowers whose
petals are strips of light
given out in a maternal
way by the earth.

HELÈNE CIXOUS

Found two lilies open in the very shallow inlet of the meadow.
Exquisitely beautiful, and unlike anything else that we have, is the first white lily
                              just expanded in some shallow lagoon where the water is leaving it
                              perfectly fresh and pure, before the insects have discovered it.

ow admirable its purity! How innocently sweet its fragrance!
ow significant that the rich, black mud of our dead stream produces
ae water-lily, – out of that fertile slime springs this spotless purity!
It is remarkable that those flowers which are most
emblematical of purity should grow in the mud.

HENRY DAVID THOREAU

The daisies grow wild
ike popcorn.

They are God's promise to the field.
How happy I am daisies, to love you.

How happy you are to be loved
and found magical, like a secret
from the sluggish field.

If all the world picked daisies
wars would end, the common cold would stop,
unemployment would end, the monetary market
would hold steady and no money would float.

ANNE SEXTON

Unloved, the *s u n -f l o w e r,* shining fair,
Ray round with flames her dusk of seed,
And many a rose-carnation feed
With summer spice the humming air;...

ALFRED, LORD TENNYSON

One flower at a time, please
however small the face.
Two flowers are one flower
too many, a d i s t r a c t i o n.
Three flowers in a vase begin
to be a little noisy.
Like cocktail conversation,
everybody t a l k i n g.
A crowd of flowers is a crowd
of flatterers *(forgive me)*.
One flower at a time. I want
to hear what it is s a y i n g.

ROBERT FRANCIS

She was standing inside the secret garden.

It was the sweetest, most mysterious-looking place anyone could imagine. The high walls which shut in were covered with the leafless stems of climbing roses, which were so thick that they were matted together. Mary Lennox knew they were roses because she had seen a great many roses in India.

All the ground was covered with grass of a wintry brown, and out it grew clumps of bushes which were surely rose-bushes if they we alive. There were numbers of standard roses which had so spread their branches that they were like little trees.

There were other trees in the garden,
nd one of the things that made the place look strangest and loveliest was that climbing roses
ad run all over them and swung down long tendrils which made light swaying curtains, and here
nd there they had caught at each other or at a far-reaching branch and had crept from one tree
o another and made lovely bridges of themselves. There was neither leaves nor roses on them now,
nd Mary did not know whether they were dead or alive, but their thin grey or brown branches and
prays looked like a sort of hazy mantle spreading over everything, walls, and trees, and even brown
rass, where they had fallen from their fastenings and run along the ground. It was this hazy tangle
rom tree to tree which made it look so mysterious.

Mary had thought it must be different from other gardens which
had not been left all by themselves so long; and, indeed, it was
different from any other place she had ever seen in her life.

FRANCES ELIZA HODGSON BURNETT

The rasping sound of a very real existence,
a very real exigency, the thrust of the bud,
he twitching erection of a bloodless stem
ust given its liquid nourishment...

       these are the spectacles and the music I came to
       respect more and more as my curiosity grew.

              Is this to say that I handle the feelings,
              the sufferings of plants with kid gloves,
              out of scrupulousness or compassion;

                     that I fret over cutting into the fiber,
                     lopping off the head, or drying up the sap? No.
                     Deeper love does not mean greater pity.

COLETTE

In joy or sadness,
flowers are our constant friends.
We eat, drink, sing, dance, and *f l i r t* with them.

KOKUZO OKAKURA

As a man and woman make
a garden between them like
a bed of stars, here
they linger in the summer evening
            and the evening turns
            cold with their terror: it
            could all end, it is capable
            of devastation. All, all
            can be lost, through scented air
                        the narrow columns
                        uselessly rising, and beyond,
                        a churning sea of poppies —
                                    Hush, beloved. It doesn't matter to me
                                    how many summers I live to return:
                                    this one summer we have entered eternity.
                                    I felt your two hands
                                    bury me to release its splendor.

                                    LOUÍSE GLÜCK

'And can all the flowers talk?'
'As well as you can,' said the Tiger-lily.
'And a great deal louder.'

Painting Credits

■

Text Credits

GE 36
Edouard Manet, Sprig of Peonies and Pruning Shears, detail, 1864, Musée d'Orsay, Paris, AR/G

GE 38
Pierre-Joseph Redouté, Rosa gallica aurelianensis, La Duchesse d'Orleans, 1817-24, AKG, Berlin

GE 39
Pierre-Joseph Redouté, Rosa Pumila, 1817-24, AKG, Berlin

GE 40
Pierre-Joseph Redouté, Rosa Indica fluenta, 1817-24, AKG, Berlin

GES 42-43
Edgar Degas, Three Dancers in Yellow Skirts, 1891, Armand Hammer Collection, Laurie Platt Winfrey, Inc.

GE 45
Gustave Caillebotte, Garden Rose and Blue Forget Me Not in a Vase, before 1879, Private Collection, Archives Gallerie Brame et Lorenceau, Paris

PAGE 46
Walter Crane, Lily of the Valley, New York Public Library

PAGE 50
German School, A Bunch of Violets, late 16th century, Graphische Sammlung Albertina, Vienna, AR/L

PAGE 52
Unknown, The Persian Prince Humay Meets the Chinese Princess Humayan in his Garden, 1420, Musée des Arts Décoratifs, Paris, AR/G

PAGE 54
R. J. Thorton, The Superb Lily Gloriosa superba, from the The Temple of Flora, 18th – 19th century, E.T. Archive

PAGE 57
Henri Matisse, Virgin and Child, 1949, Succession H. Matisse, Paris and ARS

PAGES 58-59
William Sharp, Great Water Lily, Victoria Regia, E.T. Archive

PAGE 62
Jean-François Millet, Bouquet of Daisies, 19th century, Musée du Louvre, Paris, AR

PAGE 64
Vincent van Gogh, Sunflowers, detail, 1887, Kröller-Müller Museum, Otterlo, AR/L

PAGE 66
Pieter Vanderlyn, Portrait of Deborah Glen, detail, Williamsburg, Abby Aldrich Rockefeller Folk Art Center, Williamsburg

PAGES 70-71

Marc Chagall, Blue Angel, 1937-39, Armand Hammer Collection, Laurie Platt Winfrey, Inc.

PAGE 72

J. Stella, Arthuriums in a Blue Glass Vase, 20th century, AR/Edward Owens

PAGE 74

Clare Leighton, Lily, 20th century, Courtesy of the Clare Leighton Estate

PAGE 75

Clare Leighton, Japanese Anemone, 20th century, Courtesy of the Clare Leighton Estate

PAGE 76

Unknown, Gathering Flowers, Month of April, late 15th century, Victoria & Albert Museum, London, AR/V&A

PAGE 78

Georgia O'Keeffe, Poppy, detail, 1927, oil on canvas, Museum of Fine Arts, St. Petersburg, Florida, Gift of Charles C. and Margaret Stevenson Henderson in memory of Jeanne Crawford Henderson

PAGES 80-81

Henri Matisse, Still Life with Magnolias, 1941, Musée National d'Art Moderne, Paris, AR/G/ARS

FOLLOWING CREDITS PAGE

Joseff Nigg, Floral Still Life, 19th century, Museum der Stadt Wien, Vienna, E.T. Archive

KEY TO ABBREVIATIONS

AR: Art Resource

AR/G: Art Resource/Giraudon

AR/L: Art Resource/Lessing

AR/M: Art Resource/Marburg

AR/NMAA: Art Resource/National Museum of American Art, Washington, D.C.

AR/S: Art Resource/Scala

AR/V&A: Art Resource/Victoria & Albert Museum, London

AKG: Archiv für Kunst und Geschichte

ARS: Artists Rights Society, NY

BAL: Bridgeman Art Library

Text Credits

PAGES 1 & 9
olette, *Re-Arrangements*

AGE 3
ubén Darío, *An Anthology of Spanish
etry from Garcilaso to García Lorca in
glish Translation with Spanish Originals*

AGES 6-7
ablo Neruda, *100 Love Sonnets*

AGE 12
Valt Whitman, *A Gardener's Diary*

AGE 15
oseph Addison, *The Tatler*

AGE 19
dna St. Vincent Millay, *Art & Nature*

AGES 22-23
Colette, *Journey for Myself*

AGE 25
The Odes of Solomon

AGE 27
Gertrude Jekyll, *A Celebration
of Gardens*

PAGE 28
Izumi Shikibu, *Into the Garden*

PAGES 32-33
Edith Wharton, *Italian Villas and
their Gardens*

PAGE 35
Edward Abbey, *Desert Solitaire*

PAGE 37
Colette, *Re-Arrangements*

PAGE 41
Robert Frost, *"The Rose Family"*

PAGE 44
Colette, *Re-Arrangements*

PAGE 47
Eleanour Sinclair Rohde,
The Scented Garden

PAGES 48-49
Virginia Woolf, *Mrs. Dalloway*

PAGE 51
Diane Ackerman, *A Natural History of
the Senses*

PAGE 53
Wu-men, *The Enlightened Heart*

PAGES 55 & 82
Lewis Caroll, *Through the Looking Glass*

PAGE 56
Helène Cixous, *Herbarium Verbarium*

PAGES 60-61
Henry David Thoreau, *In Wildness is the
Preservation of the World*

PAGE 63
Anne Sexton, *A Book of Women Poets
from Antiquity to Now*

PAGE 65
Alfred, Lord Tennyson, *In Memoriam*

PAGE 67
Robert Francis, *Bouquets*

PAGES 68-69
Frances Eliza Hodgson Burnett,
The Secret Garden

PAGE 73
Colette, *Re-Arrangements*

PAGE 77
Kokuzo Okakura, *The Book of Tea*

PAGE 79
Louise Glück, *The Wild Iris*

A S W A N S   I S L A N D   B O O K

Kristin Joyce is an author and book packager who produces
illustrated works for adults and children under her imprint Swans Island Books.
She has created and collaborated on over fourteen titles including this four volume
collection of select anthologies. *The Cultivated Gardener: Trees, Flowers, Fruits* and *Vegetables*
will be followed by a two-book sequel series, *The Cultivated Traveler,* in fall 1996.
Apart from books, Kristin relishes family life with her director-cinematographer
husband and their two wild and wonderful little ones. When time allows,
she swims, travels and cultivates two tiny knot gardens in Belvedere, California.

———————

Book designer Madeleine Corson has been creating
award-winning print work and packaging for over thirteen years.
She lives, works and dog walks in San Francisco.

ave Caillebotte RUBÉN DARIO Sandro Botticelli PABLO NERU

Ehret COLETTE Barbara Diestzsch WALT WHITMAN Hokusai FRANC

HODGSON BURNETT J. Stella EDNA ST. VINCENT MILLAY Jacopo Ligoz

DIXON Vincent van Gogh THE ODES OF SOLOMON Girolamo P

RUDE JEKYLL Osias Beert IZUMI SHIKIBU Hokusai EDITH WHART

uard Manet ALFRED. LORD TENNYSON Walter Crane VIRGINIA WOO

J. Thorton WU-MEN William Sharp ANNE SEXTON Jean-Franc

let EDWARD ABBEY Victor Higgins ROBERT FRANCIS Georgia O'Kee

H ADDISON W. Thorton KOKUZO OKAKURA Henri Matisse ROBERT FR

ri Fantin-Latour ELEANOUR SINCLAIR ROHDE Gustave Caillebo

E ACKERMAN Sandro Botticelli LEWIS CARROLL G. D. Ehret HEL

us Barbara Diestzsch HENRY DAVID THOREAU Henri Matisse RUE

o Sandro Botticelli PABLO NERUDA Edouard Manet COLE

tor Higgins WALT WHITMAN Hokusai FRANCES ELIZA HODGSON BURN

Stella EDNA ST VINCENT MILLAY Jacopo Ligozzi ALAN DIXON Vince

Gogh THE ODES OF SOLOMON Girolamo Pini GERTRUDE JEKYLL Os

Gustave Caillebotte RUBÉN DARÍO Sandro Botticelli PABLO NERUDA

HODGSON BURNETT J. Stella EDNA ST. VINCENT MILLAY Jacopo Ligozzi

YLL Osias Beert IZUMI SHIKIBU Hokusai EDITH WHARTON Edouar

MEN William Sharp ANNE SEXTON Jean-François Millet EDW

Thorton KOKUZO OKAKURA Georgia O'Keeffe LOUISE GLÜCK He

ustave Caillebotte DIANE ACKERMAN Sandro Botticelli LEWIS CARR

atisse RUBÉN DARÍO Vincent van Gogh PABLO NERUDA W. Thorton

RNETT J. Stella EDNA ST. VINCENT MILLAY Jacopo Ligozzi ALAN D

sias Beert IZUMI SHIKIBU Hokusai EDITH WHARTON Edouard Ma

illiam Sharp ANNE SEXTON Jean François Millet EDWARD ABBEY Vi

KUZO OKAKURA Georgia O'Keeffe LOUISE GLUCK Henri Mati

aillebotte DIANE ACKERMAN Sandro Botticelli LEWIS CARROLL G. D.

ZA HODGSON BURNETT J. Stella EDNA ST. VINCENT MILLAY Jacopo J

RTRUDE JEKYLL Osias Beert IZUMI SHIKIBU Hokusai EDITH WHAR

J. Thorton WU-MEN William Sharp ANNE SEXTON Jean Franco

EPH ADDISON W. Thorton KOKUZO OKAKURA Georgia O'Keeffe L